First published by Birch Books 2021
Western Wind Building, Juhu Tara Road, Juhu, Mumbai 400 049, India.

ISBN (978-81-947848-6-9)

birch.books

www.birchbooks.in

THE DOT STORY

BY

PEATEA &

THE GIRL

PUBLISHING PARTNER

BIRCH

BOOKS

Let's start from the start
And tell you of the great big part
The little girl had accidentally played
In getting Mr. Dot dismayed

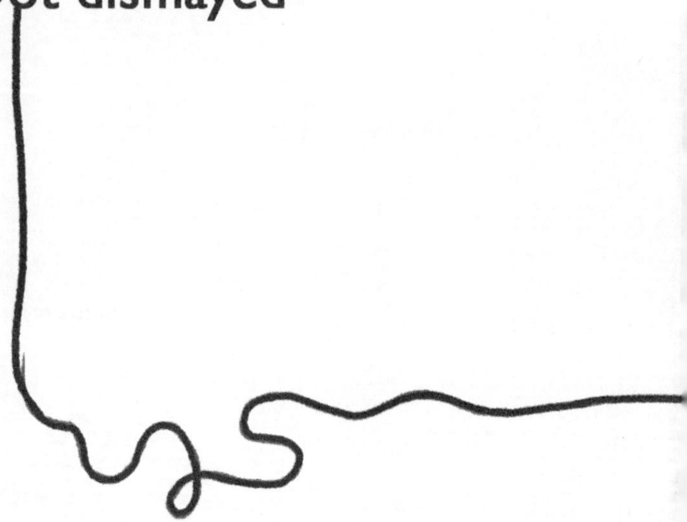

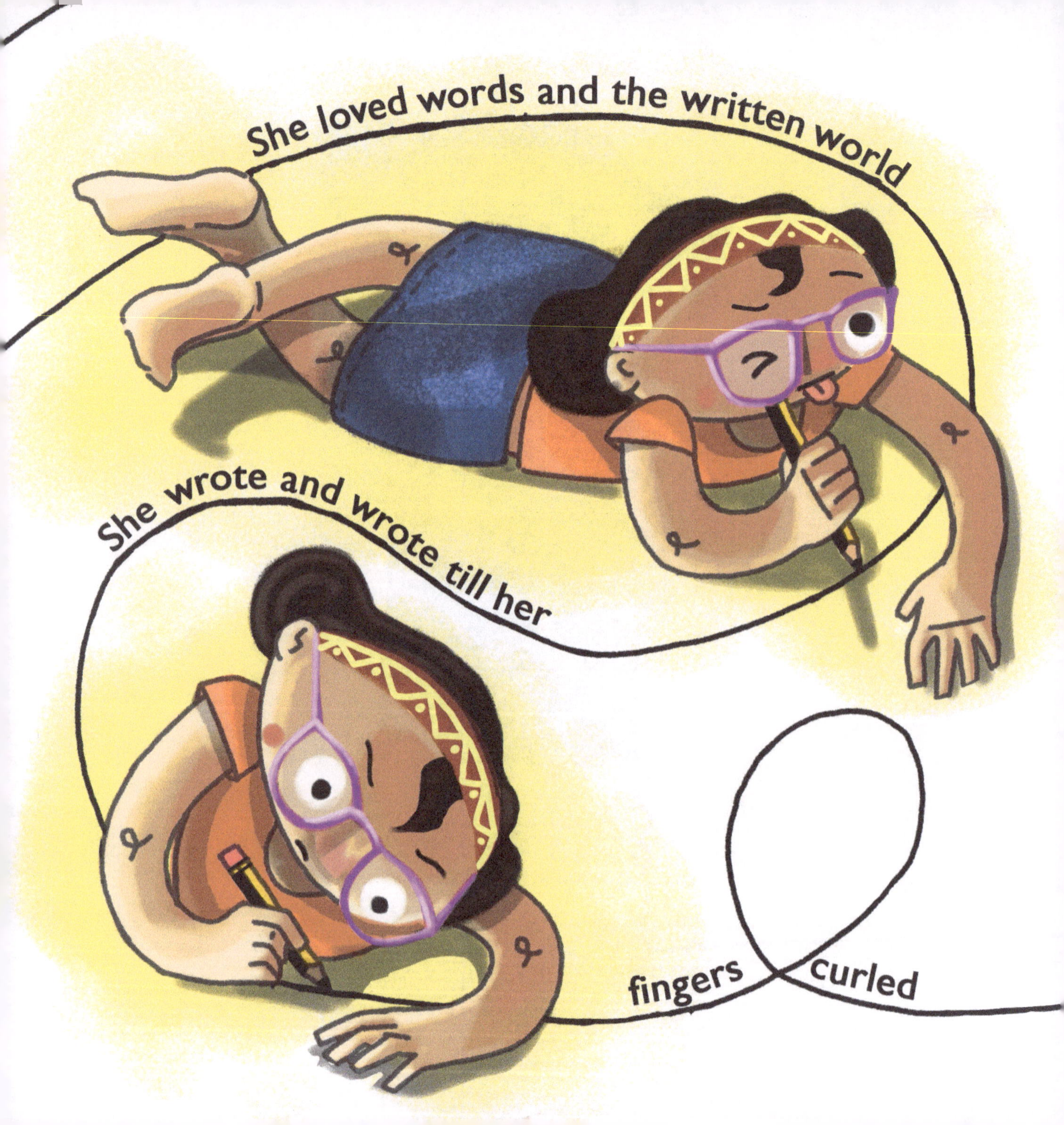

She loved words and the written world

She wrote and wrote till her fingers curled

But never once did she use
The dot to stop the flowing muse

Little did she know or care
The importance of Mr. Dot in this affair
Or that a thought becomes a complete thought
Only when you use the dot

Now who can blame Mr. Dot
The king of punctuation, for going wrought
For though he was the lord of words
Commas, hyphens and the symbol world
Here he was getting quite ignored
By a little girl to whom details bored

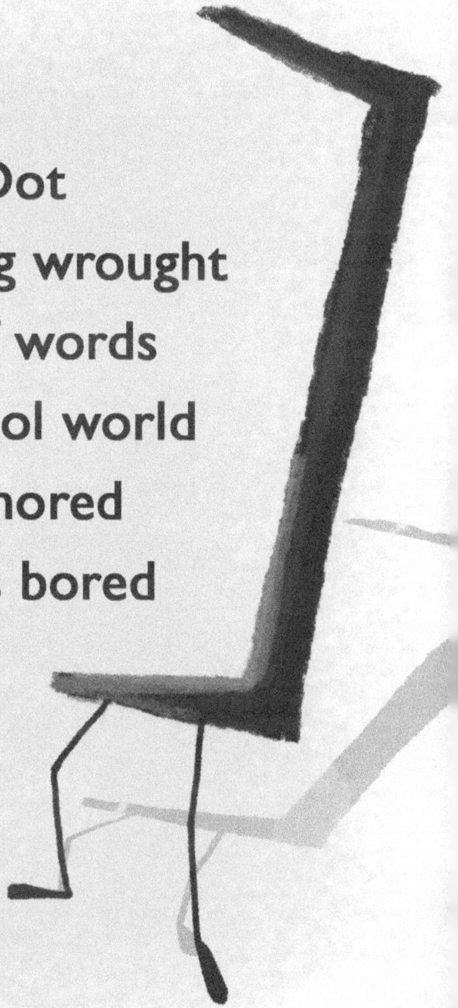

He thought it time to set things right
To gain respect and show his might
So out he jumped from the letter world
Screaming into the human world

With two commas on either side
Colon, hyphen and the rest besides
Down the table, room and hall
He went fuming, fretting and all

"I am the mighty dot!
The world's hotspot!
You think I'm small?
Oh! Not at all!
'Cause it starts with me
And ends with me
I am the only way to be!
I am the mighty dot!
The world's hotspot!
I'm here and there
I'm everywhere
This world you see
Is made of me
I am the mighty dot
The world's hotspot!"

Now all this while the girl was there
Writing more without a care
Little did she really know
That lines & letters were dots

galore.

"I call upon my brother dots
To help me teach the human lot
That no one's ever too small to ignore
That appearance don't matter more"

So one by one they left the page
Sharing Mr. Dot's outrage
Into him they flew and flew
And so Mr. Dot grew and grew

The girl noticed the page go white
A dot at a time flying by
To some place right behind her head
She turned around in utter dread

She screamed aloud in such big fear

Seeing Mr. Dot so big, so near

For he was now a great big ball
With eyes and nose and face and all

"Now do you, O little girl
Find me big enough for your world?
Or do I need to be bigger still?
To gain respect if you will!"

The girl was white stricken with fear
Her eyes were wet with great big tears

Now Mr. Dot, no wicked soul
Was sorry she was crying so

He drew her near to tell her why
You can’t ignore the litte guy
Once the girl knew her wrong
Both began to get along

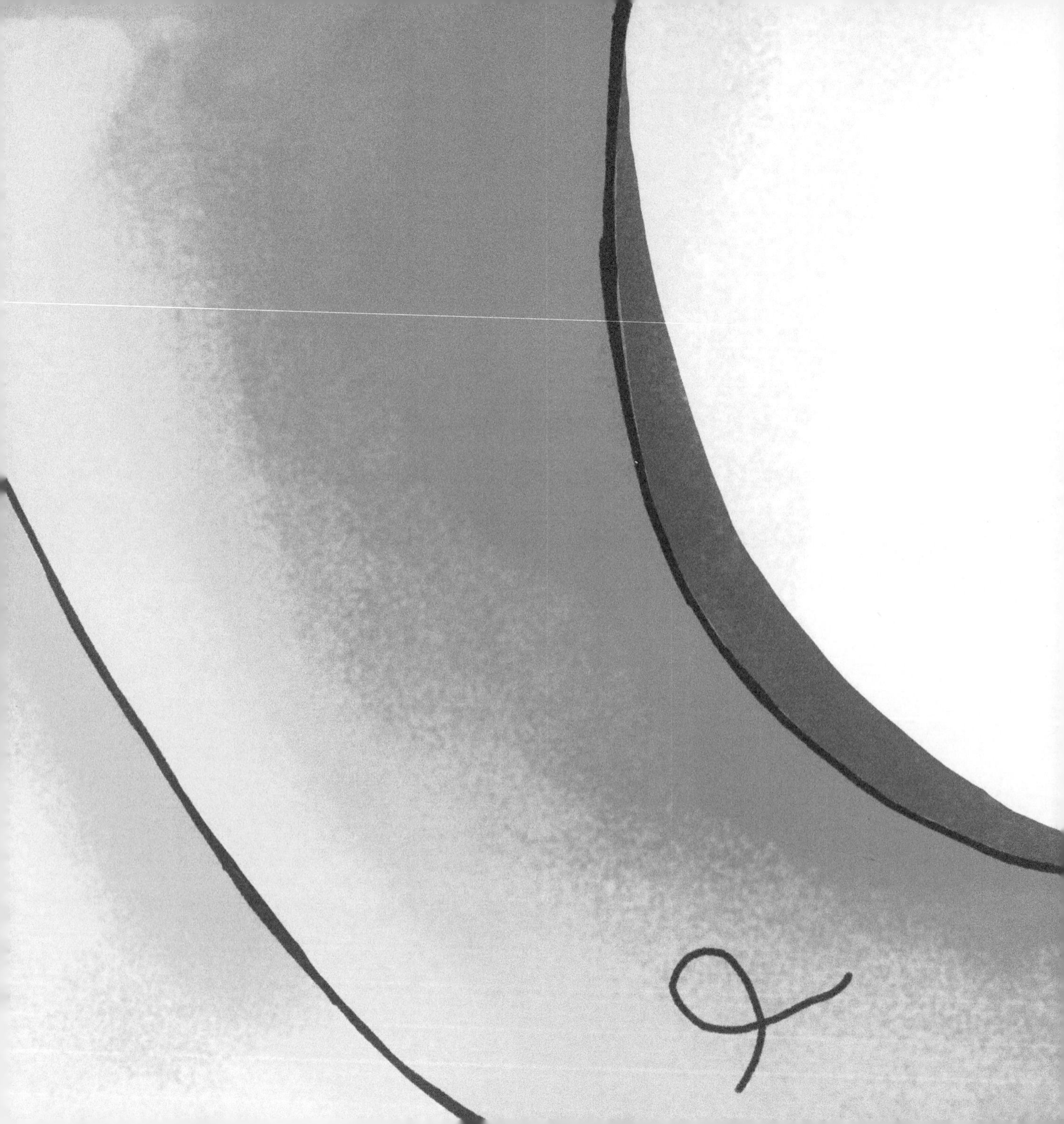

He let the dots go flying back
And fill the page as it was
Now, while writing the girl takes care
To give Mr. Dot his due share

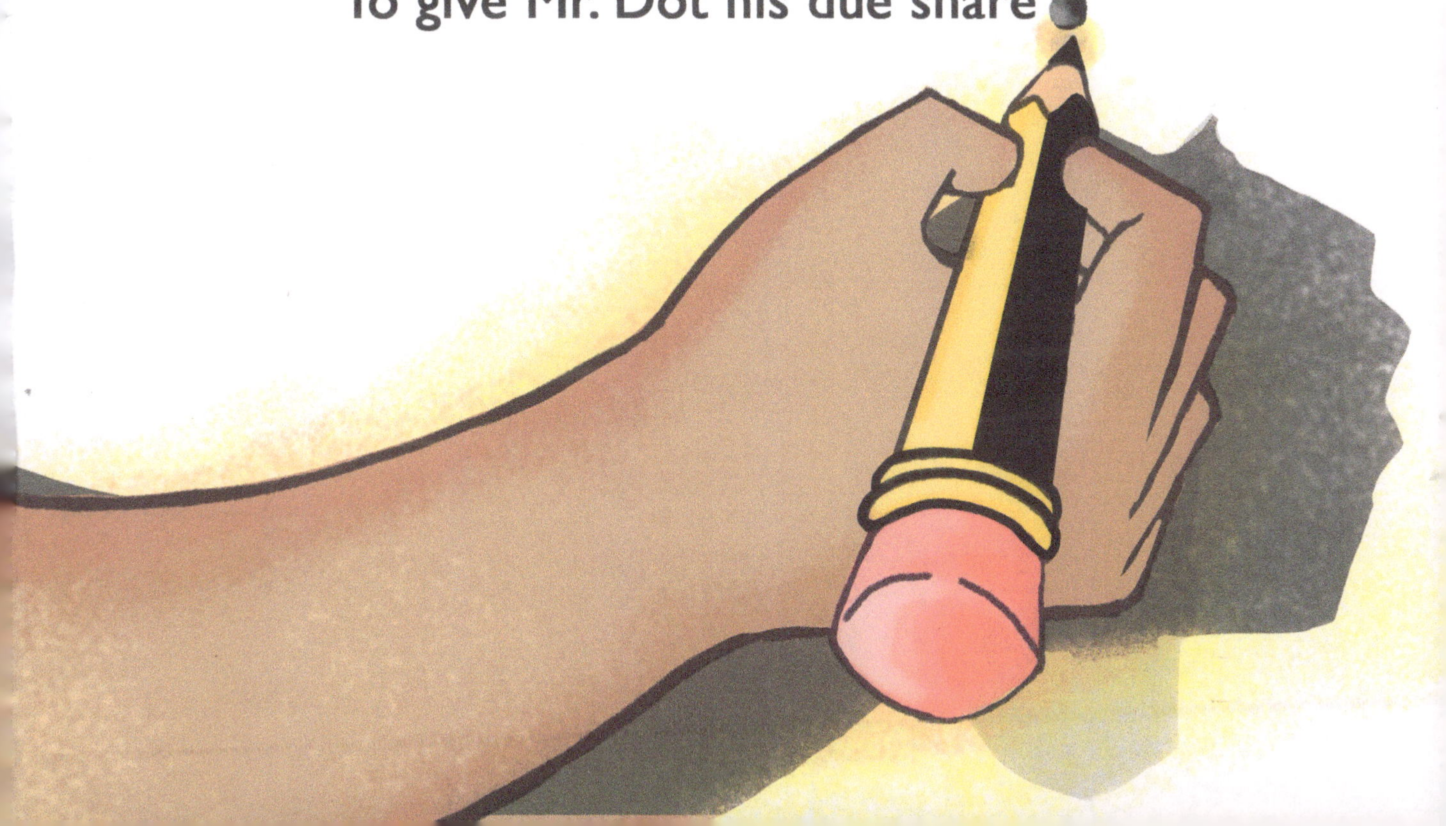